IMAGES
of America

FORT STEVENS

This granite marker was erected in 1970. It reads "On June 21, 1942, a 5.5-inch shell exploded here. One of 17 fired at Columbia River harbor defense installations by the Japanese submarine I-25. The only hostile shelling of a military base on the U.S. mainland during World War II and the first since the War of 1812." (Photograph by the author.)

ON THE COVER: Shown is a 12-inch mortar at Battery Clark in 1941. During World War I, there were eight 12-inch mortars in Battery Clark. The battery was constructed in 1899 and was inactivated on August 12, 1942. (Courtesy of the Friends of Old Fort Stevens.)

IMAGES

of America

FORT STEVENS

Susan L. Glen

ARCADIA
PUBLISHING

Published by Arcadia Publishing
Charleston, South Carolina

Printed in the United States of America

Library of Congress Catalog Card Number: 2008921576

For all general information contact Arcadia Publishing at:
Telephone 843-853-2070
Fax 843-853-0044
E-mail sales@arcadiapublishing.com
For customer service and orders:
Toll-Free 1-888-313-2665

Visit us on the Internet at www.arcadiapublishing.com

*To all who served at Fort Stevens since its construction
and to the many volunteers who continue to bring the fort to life
as part of the Oregon State Park system.*

CONTENTS

ACKNOWLEDGMENTS

This book would not have been possible without access to the many photographs from the Friends of Old Fort Stevens and the assistance of the Fort Stevens Park historian, Gale Hemmen. The Friends of Old Fort Stevens, Inc., established in 1979, is a nonprofit corporation whose mission is to support Oregon State Parks in the interpretation of Fort Stevens history and the preservation of its artifacts. Many of the pictures in their files are part of collections donated by men who were stationed at the fort and their families. Among these are albums belonging to Marshall Hanft, Sigmund Hansen, the Hampton Collection, and David Lindstrom. Pictures from the Marshall Hanft Collection, given by Erma Hanft with permission to use, included pictures from the Oregon Historical Society, the Oregon Highway Department, Ruth Milliion, and others. Most pictures in the final chapter were taken by the author.

Many of the soldiers pictured are not identified. If you know their identity, please contact the museum at Fort Stevens.

INTRODUCTION

The land upon which Fort Stevens was built originally belonged to the Clatsop Indians. They had several settlements in the area of what became Hammond, now a section of Warrenton, Oregon. A committee was appointed by the House of Representatives on December 19, 1820, to look into the settlements on the Pacific Ocean and occupation of the Columbia River. On August 5, 1851, a treaty was signed securing this land to the United States. Congress appropriated $100,000 in February 1862 for defenses at or near the mouth of the Columbia River in the Washington and Oregon Territories.

An executive order, dated February 26, 1852, reserved the present site of Fort Stevens for military purposes. Construction of the fort began in July 1863 and was completed in October 1864. In November 1864, a detachment of troops from Company A, 9th U.S. Infantry was sent to guard the fort in case of an outbreak of fighting following the reelection of U.S. president Abraham Lincoln.

The fort was named in honor of Gen. Isaac Ingalls Stevens, a governor of the Washington Territory and superintendent of Indian affairs. He was killed in action in Chantilly, Virginia, on September 1, 1862.

The original fort encompassed 2,852 acres bounded by the Pacific Ocean and the Columbia River. Today 3,700 acres make up Fort Stevens State Park, with 700 acres set aside for the historic area.

Two other forts, Fort Canby and Fort Columbia, both on the Washington side of the Columbia River, made up what was known as the Harbor Defenses of the Columbia. Construction and arming of these defenses occurred in four phases: Civil War, 1863–1866; Spanish-American War, 1898–1904; World War I, 1917–1919; and World War II, 1940–1945.

Fort Stevens was built as a walled pentagonal redoubt surrounded by a moat. There were 34 muzzle loaders of 8- and 15-inch caliber to guard the installation. The moat was filled in 1940, but the majority of the earthworks and many of the gun emplacements and buildings remain as part of the state park.

The largest gun in the earthworks in 1869 was a 15-inch smoothbore Rodman, which was fired for the first time on July 5, 1869.

U.S. president Rutherford B. Hayes visited and inspected the garrison on October 18, 1880, and four years later, the garrison was removed, and most of the fort was turned over to the U.S. Corps of Engineers for construction of the jetty. From 1884 to 1898, four successive ordnance sergeants manned the fort. A garrison detachment of one officer and 20 men was sent in March 1898 to regarrison the fort, followed by completion of the West Battery and Batteries Lewis and Walker in April. The Lewis and Walker Batteries had two 10-inch guns. In January 1899, Battery Clark was completed and armed with eight 12-inch mortars.

Although during some periods the number of soldiers at the fort was small, it continued to be garrisoned until its deactivation on January 31, 1947.

The mining of the entrance to the Columbia River occurred prior to the Spanish-American War and continued during each subsequent time of war. Fishing boats were made aware of the mine field and were able to pass without incident.

The mine casement was constructed in 1901, and the mine command was organized in 1907. The first mine target was fired by the 34th Company, Coast Artillery Corps on October 12, 1909. On July 7, 1945, orders were received to remove the Columbia River minefield.

Not included in the pictures is the Examination Artillery Battery, also known as White Evelyn. It was located on the outer portion of the South Jetty and was constructed right after the bombing at Pearl Harbor. The emplacement was not a concrete structure but was built of wood timbers and bunkers dug in the sand. Access was by the U.S. Corps of Engineers railroad, used to build the jetty. Surrounding the site were several .50- and .30-caliber machine guns.

In 1955, Fort Stevens State Park opened in the present camping area, which has been expanded in the years since. The historic area was leased from the federal government in 1967, with tours given to visitors of the main park area beginning in the summer of 1976. The following year, the historic area was opened for general day use.

Currently, reenactments of Civil War and World War II skirmishes are held at various times during the year, and the museum, located in the War Games Building, has displays relating to the history of the fort. Outside the museum is a memorial rose garden with many different varieties planted by families and friends, and tended by volunteers.

Housing that once served the officers is now privately owned but can be seen in the area outside the park, where several other buildings once part of the fort are located.

The train no longer runs, and the guns have been replaced by fiberglass replicas, but when passing through the concrete abutments, one can sense the tension that must have been felt on that night in June 1942 when the whistle of shells broke the quiet of Fort Stevens.

One

EARLY CONSTRUCTION

Shown in this official army photograph from the 1930s are the original earthworks established in the building of Fort Stevens between 1863 and 1865. On August 5, 1851, the Clatsop Indians signed a treaty with the U.S. government ceding their land for the construction of both Fort Stevens and Fort Canby on the Washington side of the Columbia River. Capt. George Elliott of the U.S. Corps of Engineers began work on the fortification in the fall of 1863. The construction consisted of raised earthworks and a moat surrounded by a glacis.

This rare photograph shows pathways of the early fort. This was enclosed by a 24-foot-high inner earthen wall and an outer 30-foot-wide ditch. U.S. president Millard Fillmore signed the executive order for the military reservations on February 26, 1852. Congress appropriated $200,000 for the defenses in the state of Oregon and Washington Territory on February 20, 1863.

On July 4, 1865, Fort Stevens was dedicated by the first fort commander, Capt. Gaston d'Artois of Company B, 8th Infantry California Volunteers. Company B was made up of 84 troops and officers. This installation existed until 1896.

The fort was built in the shape of a broad arrow and occupied about four acres. On April 9, 1865, the Civil War ended, and the fort was turned over by the U.S. Corps of Engineers to the army. None of the guns had as yet been mounted.

This 1890 picture shows the sally port, or covered entrance, into the earthworks. The entrance to the fort was across the rear ditch on a wooden bridge and through this sally port. The wooden parts and supports of the earthworks were in constant need of replacement due to rot. The sally port can still be seen in the historic area of the state park.

Inside the sally port and the earthworks were guns and piles of cannon balls. The 15-inch Rodman gun was mounted at the center. The other guns were mounted on iron carriages set on heavy timbers.

Horses were used to pull the heavy barges up onto the beach.

Horses were also used for some of the other construction projects until the trestle for the railroad was built.

Construction of Fort Stevens was originally undertaken by the U.S. Corps of Engineers. A dock needed to be built for the arrival of guns and equipment.

The mortars were brought to the fort on large rafts. The 10-inch rifled barrels on the raft were the first to arrive. When the construction was complete, one 15-inch, five 10-inch, and three 8-inch mortars were in place. The first firing of the 15-inch Rodman smoothbore cannon was on July 5, 1869.

In 1884, most of the property was turned over to the U.S. Corps of Engineers for use while they were building the jetty. A long trestle was built, and train tracks were laid on top of it.

The train carried men, equipment, and rock out to the building site.

Transportation for the U.S. Corps of Engineers out to the south jetty took a variety of forms. Also visible here is the storage and supply shack, and an area for rest, observation, and lookout.

Later the railroad brought both men and supplies to the fort.

The concrete walls of the new emplacements began to take form.

Rock and Sand Bunkers
and Mixer House
Jan. 8, 1897

This concrete mixer house was used in the construction of the West Battery in 1897 and 1898. The bunkers were made of rock and sand, and the view was up the Columbia River toward Washington.

The concrete mixer house is pictured with completed emplacements and 10-inch disappearing rifles installed.

Dumping sand
on Parados
Feb. 19, 1897

The West Battery from the beach side appeared to sit atop a large sand pile. Soldiers could observe the mouth of the Columbia River from this strategic position.

A 4-foot extension was added to the loading platforms behind the guns to provide more room for the gun crews. The last two emplacements had "all around" fire, meaning they could fire in any direction.

This is another view of the West Battery while under construction.

A disappearing carriage was installed in the pit for the mounting of a 10-inch rifle. The disappearing carriage was raised above the parapet for firing and lowered behind the parapet for protection. The recoil following discharge would return the gun to its loading position.

A 10-inch rifle sits on its emplacement atop the disappearing carriage. There were three 10-inch disappearing rifles installed. Four of the six emplacements were finished in 1898. The remaining two were completed by 1902.

The West Battery was later divided into three batteries with two guns each. They were named, from east to west, Battery Lewis, Battery Walker, and Battery Mishler. Battery Lewis, named for Capt. Merriwether Lewis of the Lewis and Clark Expedition to the Pacific Northwest, consisted of two 10-inch rifles on disappearing carriages. Battery Walker was named for Col. Leverett H. Walker, commander of Fort Stevens from April 3, 1906, to July 31, 1907. The 10-inch guns in this battery were removed in 1918. In this pre–World War I photograph, the troops sit atop one of the 10-inch guns at Battery Mishler. Battery Mishler, named for 1st Lt. Lyman Mishler, had two 10-inch guns in the ground in circular gun pits. It was the only one like it in the nation, and it was inactivated in 1918.

Battery Clark was completed in January 1899. It was named in honor of Capt. William Clark, who took part in the Lewis and Clark Expedition to the Pacific Northwest. He was appointed superintendent of Indian affairs by U.S. president James Monroe in 1822. There was a five-story command station at Battery Clark, located to the south of Swash Lake.

Lynn A. Draper stands in an observation tower, searching the horizon for the enemy. One can see seven miles out with a large telescope.

Eight 12-inch mortars were positioned in two pits, which when fired all at one time, broke windows in Seaside, Oregon, 15 miles south of the fort. In 1921, four of the mortars were removed to form Battery Guenther at Fort Canby on the Washington side of the Columbia River.

When the mortars were not in use, the barrels were lowered into a resting position.

The breech of a 12-inch mortar is pictured as it appeared when opened prior to loading a projectile. The projectile was loaded at the rear, or breech, of the mortar. The advantage to this was a reduction in reloading time.

Target practice with the 10-inch guns in Battery Russell created a large amount of smoke in the battery.

The plotting room at Battery Clark is pictured here, inside which was a large map where the plotters, wearing headsets, would mark the baseline and angles to find the triangulation for firing the projectile. Information about wind velocity, barometric pressure, and the height of the tide would be factored in to gain accuracy for the shot. The baseline was the distance between the small buildings, or base end stations.

Among those working in the mortar plotting section of Battery Clark in 1913 are (standing) Pvt. Ola Hazelbarger and Corp. Frank Harvey; (seated) ? Greenleaf, Sgt. James Hampton, and 1st Sgt. Henry M. Sellinger.

Looking at a mortar booth from the outside, the rectangular observation windows are visible.

This is a view of the inside of Battery Clark. All the batteries were concrete, with few windows and small cubical rooms.

At one time, Battery Clark was garrisoned by the 27th Artillery, shown here.

Sitting atop one of the 12-inch mortars in Battery Clark in 1912 are the following, from left to right, (first row) ? Mallicoat, Sgt. Collin's son, and James Hampton; (second row) ? Amick and ? Davis.

This picture, taken in the early days of Battery Clark, shows a sharp contrast between the service uniforms shown in the previous picture.

When the troops commenced night firing of the 12-inch mortars, the projectiles could be traced by "tracers," lights at the base of the shell. Spotting of the target and the impact of the projectile was done by listening devices and searchlights operated on shore.

The 93rd Company Police Detail assigned to Battery Clark in 1913 included, from left to right, (first row) "Jimmie" Mayfield, unidentified, "Jimmy" Gunn, James Hampton, and Corp. Edward H. Schrieber; (second row) ? Croney, unidentified, ? Marks, ? Garlock, ? Walker, "Virginia" Lee, and "Stubby" Williams; (third row) unidentified, "Curly" Holbrook, unidentified, ? Austin, George Stambook, Pete Valkenburgh, Q.M. Sgt. Luther Tingley, and Sgt. Tom Harvey.

Battery Clark was inactivated on August 12, 1942. This is how the battery appeared in 1958.

This photograph of the annual full-service practice has the soldiers putting their fingers into their ears to deaden the shock of the mortar's concussion. There were also shock resistors available for ear protection.

Battery James Pratt was built in 1900 to the right of the West Battery. It was armed with two 6-inch, disappearing carriage guns. The one is shown in 1943 prior to the battery's inactivation on August 13, 1943. The battery was named for Bvt. Capt. James Pepper Pratt of the 11th U.S. Infantry, who fought in the Civil War and was killed at Bethesda Church, Virginia.

There were 8 to 10 men on a mortar crew. This picture of a 6-inch gun, taken in about 1943, includes, from left to right, ? Greenleaf, "Count Fewclothes," Corp. Tom Harvey, ? Van, Pvt. Ola Hazelbarger, James Hampton, and 1st. Sgt. Henry M. Sellinger.

Shown here are command sections 2 and 4 at the West Battery and Battery Pratt. Battery Pratt was modernized in 1945 to protect the minefields.

Battery Constant Freeman was built within the earthworks. Colonel Freeman fought in the Revolutionary War and the War of 1812. Battery Freeman was leveled in 1940 to create the lower parade ground.

Shown here is a gun pintal, left, from the Civil War Era. This was the pin on which the gun carriage revolved. In 1940, Battery Freeman was blown up, and, along with the earthworks, the area was flattened and provided space for tents and a parade ground.

Battery Freeman had two 6-inch rapid-fire guns on barbette carriages and one 3-inch rapid-fire gun on a pedestal mount, as shown here.

The added shield on the gun was to protect the crew from the blast created when the gun was fired.

This is the emplacement for the 3-inch rapid-fire gun. The guns were dismounted in 1917.

On August 12, 1904, Battery Russell, named for Bvt. Maj. Gen. David A. Russell, was completed with two 10-inch disappearing rifles. Battery Russell was the first section to be opened to the public.

The 10-inch rifles in this battery were also breech-loading, as shown in this photograph.

The barrel of a 10-inch mortar is waiting to be positioned on its carriage.

Soldiers wait with shells and shell trays to be loaded into the 10-inch disappearing rifles at Battery Russell.

Battery Russell was at the right foot of Fire Control Hill. It was the last 10-inch battery of this type to remain active in the United States.

Walking along the escarpments in Battery Russell, the ocean is visible. The effective range for the guns at this battery was 14,000 yards. Adjustments could be made to the projectiles to attain greater range.

Pictured is one of the counterweight pits in Battery Russell, where the gun carriages were mounted in 1905 and the guns placed in 1907.

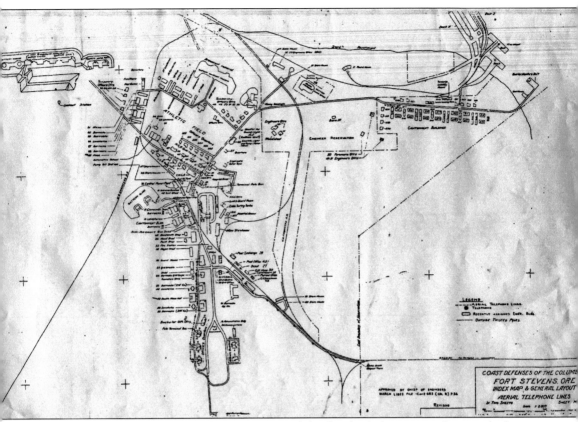

This is a March 1, 1922, map of Fort Stevens made by the chief of engineers, showing the location of all the buildings and batteries on the fort at that time.

Two

SUBMARINE MINES

In April 1898, the submarine mine casement was completed. Mines were laid in the entrance to the Columbia River using many different ships. In August 1941, the mine planter, Lt. Col. Ellery W. Niles, arrived from Fort Winfield Scott in California. The mine command was organized in 1907.

Life aboard the mine-laying ship was task-ridden and dangerous once the firing mechanism was installed. Shown here is the crews mess aboard a mine layer.

The Coast Artillery Corps was created for the purpose of laying mines. Mines were loaded with TNT, the standard explosive charge being 1,200 pounds, and placed aboard the ships to be planted in nets in the river. Gun cotton pellets were used as the explosive charge. The fulminate of mercury firing mechanism was inserted just before planting.

Cables were attached and carried by a mine yawl to the shore, where they were connected to the control room. The mine yawl was also used to show the mines' position for the charts in the control room. One mine yawl in use at the fort measured 26 feet.

Right after the attack on Ft. Stevens by a Japanese submarine, a field command post was set up. Shown here are the Harbor Defenses of the Columbia command personnel getting reports concerning the shell craters..

Mine-planting operations in 1898 were carried out by the U.S. Corps of Engineers. No mines were planted during the Spanish-American War.

A mine casement was also constructed across the river at Fort Columbia. In 1918, the original sand-covered casemate was given a cement facing. Mines were anchored to the river bottom to keep them from drifting.

The U.S. Army began control of the operation of the submarine mine program in April 1901. Fort Stevens remained the control center until 1937, when it was transferred to Fort Columbia. Planting operations remained at Fort Stevens.

During May and June 1918, troops practiced laying electrical cable in the river, planting mines, and retrieving them. World War I ended in November 1918, and mine practice was again limited. Shown here is mine firing practice in 1941.

New mines that lay on the bottom of the river rather than floating near the surface were used in World War II. An underwater audio-reception system was also installed.

In July 1945, the order to remove the mines from the Columbia River was received. Battery B, 249th Coast Artillery was assigned to mine recovery, which continued until 1947.

Three

PETER IREDALE

The *Peter Iredale* was a four-masted steel barque that ran aground on October 25, 1906, at Clatsop Beach off Fort Stevens.

A crew was sent out from the Point Adams Lifeboat Station. The lighthouse, shown here, was built in 1875, was replaced by the *Columbia Lightship* (a U.S. Coast Guard vessel stationed at the mouth of the Columbia River) in 1892, and was destroyed in 1912 with the building of the south jetty. The lighthouse stood near the location of Battery Russell, one mile south of Point Adams, and was a redwood Victorian structure. H. C. Tracy was the first lighthouse keeper.

Built in June 1890 at Maryport, England, the ship belonged to Peter Iredale and John Porter. The ship weighed 2,075 tons and carried a crew of 25 plus two stowaways. The captain was H. Lawrence. After the rescue of all aboard, the captain made a final toast to his ship, "May God bless you, and may your bones bleach in the sands." The ship's bones remain, although time and tides have hidden much.

A barque is defined as a ship with three or more masts with square sails on all except the mizzen, or aft, which is fore-and-aft rigged.

The ship was 285 feet long, fashioned from steel plates on an iron frame. Sections of the frame become visible from time to time, providing an area tourist attraction.

After the sailors were evacuated by lifeboat, they were tended to at Fort Stevens. Although plans were made to tow the ship back out to sea, weeks of bad weather caused the ship to list to the right and become embedded in the sand, where it has remained. The amount of the old ship that is visible depends on the severity of the winter storms.

On occasion, the troops pitched their tents on the beach beside the wreck. The wreck is within Fort Stevens State Park and is part of the Lewis and Clark National and State Historical Parks.

During World War II, when a Japanese submarine fired shells at Battery Russell, the wreck was in the line of fire but was unscathed. The wreck was entwined in barbed wire the day after the shelling. It remained as such until the end of the war. Thirty-four linear miles of barbed wire were placed around strategic points of the harbor defenses. A machine gun nest was maintained on the beach near the wreck.

The British vice-consulate held a naval court of inquiry in Astoria, Oregon, on November 12 and 13, 1906, to determine the cause of the wreck. Following the investigation, no blame was placed on Capt. H. Lawrence or his crew for the wreck. The court also put on record their appreciation for the prompt action of the U.S. lifesaving crew at Hammond and the action of the commander, Col. Leverett H. Walker, the U.S. Army, and his officers and men at Fort Stevens.

The *Peter Iredale* was used as a backdrop for advertising photographs, such as this one for visiting the Oregon Coast. The side of the airplane notes 400 miles of scenic coastline.

Four

PRE–WORLD WAR I AND THE WAR YEARS

The gate into Fort Stevens is marked by two tall concrete blocks. The United States declared war on Germany on April 6, 1917. Fort Stevens served as a staging area for training new artillery units.

This field piece was fired for reveille, retreat, and special occasions. One story is that when it was near the guardhouse, its firings disturbed two mules in a pasture, so it had to be moved to just inside the main gate. This salute gun fired black powder.

The saluting gun was used to answer salutes from ships passing in the Columbia River. An M 1902 three-inch gun on a carriage was a common field gun. A noncommissioned officer and two privates made up the detail for firing of the salute gun. The noncommissioned officer marched the detachment to and from the gun, which was fired and sponged under his direction.

This 3.2-inch 75-millimeter gun was used around 1937. The gun was on a carriage to allow for mobility and was fitted with a shield to protect the firing crew from rifle fire and muzzle blast.

Firing of the gun was done several times a day, in addition to those firings for ceremonial occasions.

Model 1903 Springfield .30-caliber bolt-action rifles are stacked, ready to be retrieved for duty. This was an American magazine-fed bolt-action rifle used during the early 20th century.

At the beginning of World War I, guns were also placed aboard railway cars. These were called railway mortars. The gun carriage revolved on an axis and turned the gun with it. A special pedestal mount allowed for a 360-degree traverse. The guns were mounted on three standard railway artillery cars designed by the Ordnance Department for 7-inch and 8-inch guns or 12-inch mortars, as on the car in this photograph.

Among those standing in front of the headquarters of the Harbor Defenses of the Columbia building are Captain Napier, Larry Morgan, Colonel Aklsey, Col. Carl C. Doney, and Colonel Knapp. A Coast Artillery Corps officer's training school was located at Fort Stevens at the outset of World War I.

In front of the headquarters building are cannons from the Spanish-American War. The inscription on the cannons reads: "Agraciado (Graceful) / Cast in Seville, Spain 1783 / Mounted at Fort Santiago Manila / During the Spanish Occupation of the Philippine Islands / Mounted at Fort Stevens, Nov. 1944."

The brick guardhouse was built in 1911 at a cost of more than $20,000. It still stands today outside the fenced historic area. It usually held 5 to 6 prisoners but could hold up to 12. The building was heated by a hot water system with the furnace in the basement, and there was a planked street in front.

A guard mount stands for inspection under the direction of Col. Ed Farnsworth. A guard mount is the military formation that security members attend before going to their posts. It is a combination of roll call and instructions or briefings.

The interior of the guardhouse is pictured here. This was the headquarters of the interior guard sentinels. Each stood a two-hour tour, with a four-hour rest. The guards marched in front of the building except when it was raining. Rain brought the guards up onto the porch to march from reveille to retreat.

The guardhouse had cells for prisoners.

Looking out the window of the guardhouse in 1958, about nine years after the fort's closure, a school bus can be seen passing one of the many units of officer housing.

Baseball was an active pastime at the fort. Shown here is a baseball team from 1912.

Baseball games were played against other local teams on the field. This game of Fort Stevens versus the militia occurred in August 1912. In the background are several buildings, including one tall platform.

Football was also played by many of the service personnel.

Indoor activities included the occasional game of pool in the day room in the old 93rd. Pictured from left to right are ? Schreiber, "Slim," and James Hampton.

A friendly game of cards is played around 1912 in the squad room by, from left to right, ? Kunz, "Mutt" Banks, ? McCauley, the daughter of one of the soldiers, and "Sloppy" Thomas.

Troops are shown in front of the theater in this picture from May 1913.

This later picture shows a theater building that also included a bowling alley.

Holidays were a lonesome time for soldiers away from home. Meals were especially important to the morale of the troops.

The folder for the menu for Thanksgiving dinner in 1917 has an eagle and three flags on its cover.

Menu

Cream of Oyster Soup

Crisped Celery   Ripe Olives

Sliced Tomatoes

Stuffed Young Turkey, Oyster Dressing

Cranberry and Apple Sauce

Giblet Gravy

Creamed Mashed Potatoes

Creamed Sweet Peas

Mince Pie   Pumpkin Pie

Layer Cake   Mixed Nuts

Apples   Oranges   Bananas   Grapes

Tea   Coffee

Cigars   Cigarettes

Shown here is the menu for Thanksgiving dinner in November 1917.

ROSTER of ELEVENTH CO. O. C. A.

CAPTAIN
Fred K. Gettins

2ND LIEUTENANTS
James H. Mills
Lewis C. Beebe

1ST SERGEANT
Fisher, Ben S.

SUPPLY SERGEANT
Cushing, Leonard G.

MESS SERGEANT
Painter, Ferdinand M.

SERGEANTS
McLeod, Walter S.
Hibarger, Carl F.
Grimes, Thayer
Dillard, Robert C.
Goodrum, William
Ferguson, Duncan
McInturff, John W.
Merchant, James M.

CORPORALS
Jensen, Charles A.
Carlson, Clifford M.
McGeorge, Ronald A.
Adams, Milton R.
Pratt, Hermann L.
Fensler, Clarke W.
Ferguson, John
Dement, Harry G.
Norback, Gosta
Molony, James L.
Busch, Robert C.
Kinney, Orley E.

COOKS
Bargelt, Harold L.
Sicardo, John

MECHANICS
Cooley, Loran D.
Robinett, Clarence B.

BUGLER
Taylor, Charles A.

PRIVATES, 1ST CLASS
Cook, John E.
Goodman, Duane C.
Graham, George D.
Hermance, Clyde R.
Hinze, George E.
Lando, Charles I.
Leavens, James M.
Megale, Antonio
Neilson, Alexander G.
Petersen, Holger V.
Pinkerton, Ray R.
Ray, Robert
Tacha, Claude W.
Torrey, Guy C.
Wooley, Jesse W.
Wright, Charner L.

PRIVATES
Armstrong, Wilfred W.
Bargelt, Hallet C.
Bargelt, Paul J.
Busch, Albert H.
Carl, Henry
Childreth, Graydon E.
Claxton, George R.
Collier, Jack
Cope, William E.
Daigle, Arthur
Douglas, Duncan E.
Dubuque, Louis D.
Frantz, Jesse D.
Garrett, Bonner
George, Elias P.
Gray, Gilbert E.
Greene, Forrest B.
Haines, Harold P.
Hale, Earl L.
Hanson, Vernon H.
Hendee, Harold G.
Henderson, Carl W.
Hill, Oliver E.
Hillman, William
Horton, Louis H.
Judd, Wendell B.
Lane, Cash R.
Lecocq, Henry
Miller, Harley N.
Moyer, John S.
McLain, Wilfred
McLyman, John W.
Oberst, George L.
Olsen, William F.
Painter, Wayne
Pratt, Percy J.
Robertson, Herschel
Russell, Ronald C.
Russell, Samuel F.
Smith, Hazard A.
Starr, Chester C.
Sydnam, Charles
Tompkins, Lloyd J.
Treadgold, Frederic V.
Tribbey, Bert M.
Turnham, Bryan
Volz, John
Walter, Festus C.
Weekly, Smith A.
Wirostek, Joseph A.
Wooden, Robert P.
Wroe, Floyd A.

Included on the back of the menu is the roster of troops in 11th Company Oregon Coast Artillery.

Christmas dinner was enjoyed in 1912 in the 93rd Company's mess hall. Facing the camera are James Hall and "Wagon" Harris.

In 1912, in another dining hall, the 160th Company enjoys their Christmas dinner. "Billy" Cross and Russ are on the right facing the table.

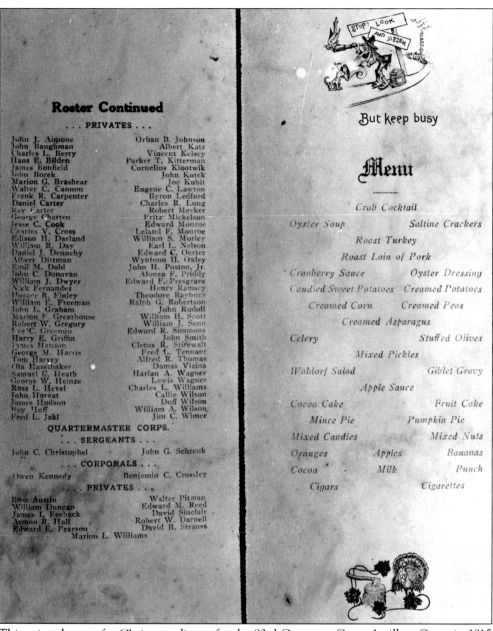

Roster Continued

... PRIVATES ...

John J. Aimone	Orban B. Johnson
John Baughman	Albert Katz
Charles L. Berry	Vincent Kelsey
Hans E. Bilden	Parker T. Kitterman
James Bonfield	Cornelius Klootwik
John Borek	John Kotek
Marion G. Brashear	Joe Kubit
Walter C. Cannon	Eugene C. Lawton
Frank R. Carpenter	Byron Ledford
Daniel Carter	Charles R. Long
Roy Carter	Robert Meeker
George Chatten	Fritz Mickelson
Jesse C. Cook	Edward Monroe
Charles V. Cross	Leland F. Monroe
Edison H. Darland	William S. Morley
William R. Day	Earl L. Nelson
Daniel J. Dennehy	Edward C. Oerter
Albert Dittman	Wyntoun H. Oxley
Emil M. Dold	John H. Poston, Jr.
John C. Donovan	Alonzo F. Priddy
William J. Dwyer	Edward F. Presgrave
Nick Fernandez	Henry Ramsey
Horace R. Finley	Theodore Rayburn
William E. Freeman	Ralph G. Robertson
John L. Graham	John Rudolf
Marion F. Greathouse	William H. Scott
Robert W. Gregory	William J. Senn
Lee C. Greenup	Edward R. Simmons
Harry E. Griffin	John Smith
James Hanson	Cletus R. Stirewalt
George M. Harris	Fred L. Tennant
Tom Harvey	Alfred R. Thomas
Ola Hazelbaker	Damas Vizina
Samuel C. Heath	Harlan A. Wagner
George W. Heinze	Lewis Wagner
Ross L. Hevel	Charles L. Williams
John Horvat	Callie Wilson
James Hudson	Doff Wilson
Roy Huff	William A. Wilson
Fred L. Jakl	Jim C. Wimer

QUARTERMASTER CORPS.

... SERGEANTS ...

John C. Christophel	John G. Schrenk

... CORPORALS ...

Owen Kennedy	Benjamin C. Crossley

... PRIVATES ...

Ross Austin	Walter Pitman
William Duncan	Edward M. Reed
James I. Feeback	David Sinclair
Armon R. Hall	Robert W. Darnell
Edward E. Pearson	David B. Strauss
Marion L. Williams	

But keep busy

Menu

Crab Cocktail

Oyster Soup	Saltine Crackers

Roast Turkey

Roast Loin of Pork

Cranberry Sauce	Oyster Dressing

Candied Sweet Potatoes   Creamed Potatoes

Creamed Corn	Creamed Peas

Creamed Asparagus

Celery	Stuffed Olives

Mixed Pickles

Waldorf Salad	Giblet Gravy

Apple Sauce

Cocoa Cake	Fruit Cake
Mince Pie	Pumpkin Pie
Mixed Candies	Mixed Nuts
Oranges	Apples	Bananas
Cocoa	Milk	Punch
Cigars	Cigarettes	

This printed menu for Christmas dinner for the 93rd Company Coast Artillery Corps in 1915 survived as a keepsake following World War I.

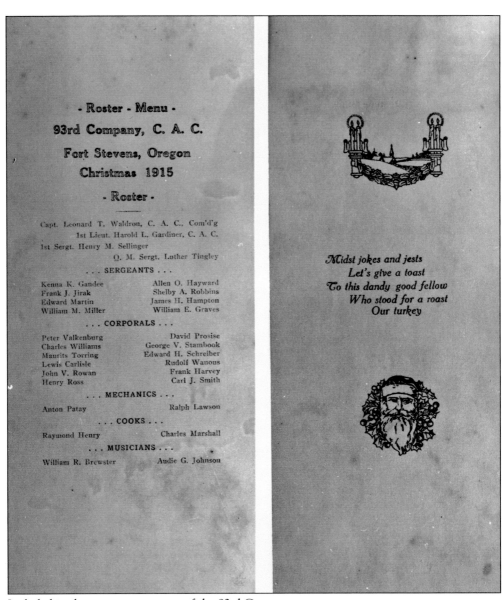

- Roster - Menu -

93rd Company, C. A. C.

Fort Stevens, Oregon

Christmas 1915

- Roster -

Capt. Leonard T. Waldron, C. A. C., Com'd'g
1st Lieut. Harold L. Gardiner, C. A. C.
1st Sergt. Henry M. Sellinger
Q. M. Sergt. Luther Tingley

... SERGEANTS ...

Kenna K. Gandee   Allen O. Hayward
Frank J. Jirak   Shelby A. Robbins
Edward Martin   James H. Hampton
William M. Miller   William E. Graves

... CORPORALS ...

Peter Valkenburg   David Prosise
Charles Williams   George V. Stambook
Maurits Torring   Edward H. Schreiber
Lewis Carlisle   Rudolf Wanous
John V. Rowan   Frank Harvey
Henry Ross   Carl J. Smith

... MECHANICS ...

Anton Patay   Ralph Lawson

... COOKS ...

Raymond Henry   Charles Marshall

... MUSICIANS ...

William R. Brewster   Audie G. Johnson

*Midst jokes and jests
Let's give a toast
To this dandy good fellow
Who stood for a roast
Our turkey*

Included in the menu was a roster of the 93rd Company.

In the years before World War I, other buildings were constructed at Fort Stevens. The stables, located near the train station and guardhouse, housed the horses used to haul cannons and other items in the early construction of the fort.

The first post exchange is shown with a large clock on the front.

Another post exchange was constructed in 1941. In the basement of the exchange was a restaurant and common area. Past and present activities were discussed over a glass of the 3.2-percent beer sold here.

The troops would erect their tents on the field, as seen in this photograph of the Oregon National Guard. The tents were canvas and conical in shape. They were erected on the earthworks by Battery Freeman.

Here is a close-up view of this style of tent from 1916.

Tents came in many styles and sizes. Here the troops are shown in a pre–World War I bivouac.
A bivouac is a military encampment made with tents.

Pup tents were also set up for inspection. Each tent was for two soldiers.

The inspecting officer walked the length of the formation, checking each tent and the layout of the soldier's gear.

The soldiers stood beside their tent and gear. At the outset of World War I, there was not enough housing for about 1,200 men and officers, and they were still sleeping in tents. With only one uniform and one pair of shoes, which were often rain-soaked, they sometimes had to sit in their underwear waiting for their uniforms to dry.

All of a soldier's gear had to be laid out in front of the tent in a specified order.

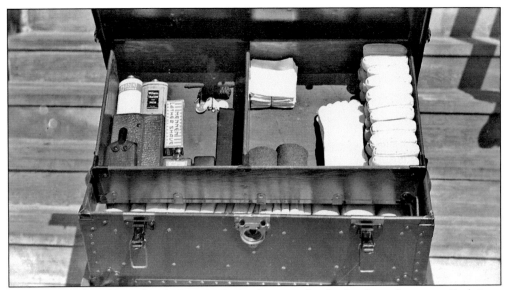

The items in the soldier's foot locker also had a designated order for their placement. Each item also had a specific way in which it was folded.

At the end of the inspection, the order was given to strike tents, and the tents would come down.

The Civilian Conservation Corps was housed on the base from 1935 to 1937 while they worked on soil conservation, forest firefighting, and control of the shifting sand on the beaches. They also assisted in the effort to restore historic structures.

Officers' housing was located away from the batteries but near the guardhouse, theater, and stables.

Some of the buildings on the 18th Coast Artillery Parade Ground are identified from left to right as follows: (2) nurse's quarters, (3) headquarters battery office, (4) noncommissioned officers' barracks, (5) headquarters battery barracks, (6) Company B battery barracks, (7) headquarters battery barracks, (8) quartermaster's building, and (10) baseball diamond.

The wooden buildings required constant care. Scaffolding surrounds a barracks that is being painted.

This is the receiving barracks. Troops checked in here upon arriving at the fort.

Sleeping inside the barracks was a big improvement over sleeping in a tent. This picture of the squad room for Battery E, 3rd Coast Artillery shows the cots all made up identically.

The quartermaster is an individual or unit that is responsible for supplies and provisions for the troops. This is the quartermaster's barracks.

Pictured is the barracks home of the 93rd Coast Artillery Company in 1913. The shrubbery and grass lawn were usually maintained by the "naughty boys," soldiers who had "stepped the boundary lines of good discipline" and were assigned to the "dandelion pulling detail." Next door is the barracks that Battery E of the 3rd Coast Artillery called home while stationed at the fort.

The 34th Company stands outside their barracks in 1913 or 1914. Concrete walks had not been installed yet. The group appears in two different uniforms. The detail on the left is in service olive drabs, and the detail on the right is wearing dress blues.

Post headquarters are pictured in the earlier years. Buildings were torn down and rebuilt as the need arose. Sometimes they were built in the same location as a previous building for the same use, but they were often built in different locations entirely.

This sign was posted outside the mess area at Battery Russell in 1942.

Kitchen duty, known as KP, was shared by all. Trained cooks prepared the meals. Here a cook prepares one of the three daily meals.

Soldiers standing KP duty were assigned the tasks of pealing spuds (potatoes), washing dishes, and other related tasks.

Troops from Fort Stevens marched in the Regatta Parade in Astoria. This picture is from about 1913. The military was highly regarded by the local population, and they were invited to parade at various times in all the local communities.

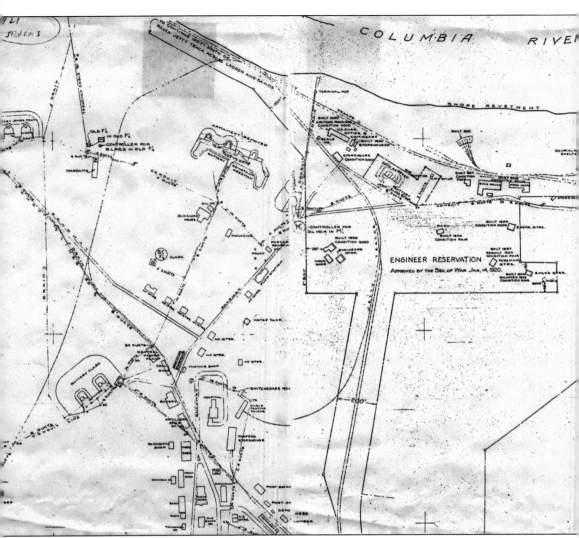

This 1920 map shows the location of many of the buildings as they were during World War I. Many of the foundations can still be seen, but the majority of the wooden buildings are gone.

Five

WORLD WAR II

Old Glory flies over the field outside one garrison on July 4, 1945, at Fort Stevens. It is a 48-star flag, as neither Hawaii nor Alaska had become states before the fort was deactivated.

Arrival of trainload of selectees from Ohio at Ft Stevens, Oct 1941

Troops arrived by train at the railroad station located near the guardhouse and the gymnasium. This area is outside the historic area of the park.

World War II brought the reactivation of many units of the Oregon National Guard into active duty with the U.S. Army. The troops came to Fort Stevens for training before being shipped to duty stations overseas.

A troop transport truck enters the gate at Fort Stevens. The tall, white, cement blocks still stand at the entrance to the fort as part of the Oregon State Park System. A second set, unpainted, mark the entrance to the historic park.

The soldiers came in all sizes. In 1940, the Selective Service required all men between the ages of 21 and 30 to register for the draft. When the United States entered World War II, all men aged 18 to 65 had to register, but only those aged 18 to 45 were made liable for the draft.

Selectees from the 249th Coast Artillery Regiment of the Oregon National Guard are shown standing in formation outside the barracks in 1941. They were ordered into active military service on September 16, 1940.

This is the unit flag for the 249th. The background was red with the wording and insignia in yellow. All units of the 249th were first stationed at Fort Stevens before some detachments were sent to Fort Canby and Fort Columbia.

More construction was undertaken on the fort grounds from 1941 to 1943 to provide additional housing for the increase in units, as well as other support structures.

Fort Stevens is pictured as it appeared in early 1941. This view looks north from the water tower.

Water was provided for the fort from a large water tower. One water tower was south of the new officer's quarters. The wooden water tower held 60,000 gallons of water. Another steel tank had a capacity of 150,000 gallons.

The water tower fell to the ravages of time and weather. The 35-foot-tall tower stood at an elevation of 127 feet above mean water level. The height was necessary to provide water pressure at the faucets.

Among the other buildings added during this time were a recreation hall, noncommissioned officers' garages, an indoor rifle range, a regimental storehouse, and a ferry waiting and baggage room.

Additional officers' quarters with mess facilities, a nurses' quarters, and an officers' club were included in the new construction.

The meteorological station shown in this 1940 photograph is no longer in existence. This was where information was gathered to make predictions about the weather. The weather played a major role in plotting the trajectory of projectiles fired from the batteries.

The National Guard band arrived from Coos Bay to be stationed at Battery Russell in 1940. In 1941, they were told they had to stay another year. They fell into formation in their underwear, and when asked why, band director CWO Walter Charles Germain quoted the regulation that said "boots, regulation belts, hats, and their instruments."

The band made the protest an annual event but routinely appeared in complete uniform for many events, as seen here in formation in 1943. This band was also requested to play at other events throughout the state.

This 1941 Sperry Controller was operated by three men. It was used to manually operate the Sperry searchlight by remote control. Because of its brightness and for safety, as it made a good target, it was placed several hundred feet from the searchlight. The searchlight had 800 million candlepower.

This Sperry searchlight was one of 10,000 carbon arc searchlights built by Sperry Gyroscope and General Electric for the U.S. military as antiaircraft searchlights for spotting enemy aircraft during the night. The light operated on 78 volts of direct current at 150 amps. Production was stopped in 1944, when the searchlights were replaced by radar.

The carbon arc searchlight was developed by Elmer A. Sperry in 1918. In addition to spotting aircraft at night, it was also used for the illumination of battlefields for night attacks, for signaling, and was fitted to tanks, where it was used for blinding the enemy. One of these searchlights remains on display at Fort Stevens.

Power for the searchlight was provided by a movable gasoline power plant. Also built by Sperry Gyroscope, the combined weight of the light and power plant was about 6,000 pounds. It was operated by a Hercules JDX 6-cylinder flat-head. It was water cooled and ran at 1,150 revolutions per minute.

This sound locator, also made by Sperry, was used to detect airplanes at a distance at night. The "horns" gathered and amplified the sound, which could then be heard through a stethoscope device worn by the operators. One operator listened to the left and right horn to obtain the direction of the airplane, while the other operator listened to the top and bottom horns to ascertain the elevation of the incoming airplane.

Before the invention of radar, the sound locator was the most practical way of detecting airplanes at night by listening for the noise of their engines. Sperry invented and manufactured these devises from 1939 to 1945. More than 77,000 military personnel were trained in their use.

Another piece of equipment, invented and developed by Ambrose Swasey, was the Swasey Depression Range and Position Finder, which was used for determining the range from the observer to any distant object. The instrument could determine the position of an object with respect to any place or line.

A simulated gas attack was carried out on the south jetty. Children living on the base carried gas masks to school and had been instructed in their use.

In the early years, children attended school on base or in Hammond. Shown here is a school group from 1917. Pictured from left to right are (first row) Albin Oman, Tom Falconer, unidentified, Cecil Saunders, Lulu Poaso, Helen Glanz, and Blanch Anderson; (second row) unidentified, Douglas Cauley, Peg Keck, Bertha Johnson, Frieda Johnson, unidentified, and Nellie Fuinn; (third row) Johnny McDermott, Prof. Walter R. McClure, and Hollis Stoddard.

Camouflage nets were used to cover the batteries, housing, and gun emplacements to prevent aerial detection. Artificial trees were positioned, dummy houses were built, and artificial sod and other types of natural vegetation were used to conceal the fort. Paint was used to change the camouflage with the change of the seasons and to adapt it to the area. Dummy gun batteries were also constructed.

The area around Fort Stevens consists of sand dunes, scrub pine, beach grass, and swamp. Coloring changes from the lush green of summer to a dull brown in the winter.

Medical and dental care was carried out at the hospital on base. Doctors, dentists, and nurses were also part of the army and were assigned to duty at Fort Stevens. This patient needed some dental work done.

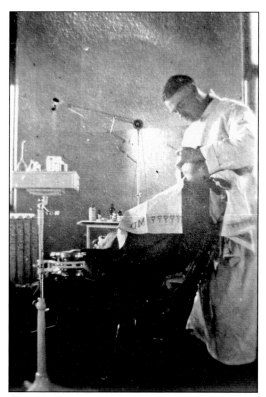

Dr. Paul Walker, upper right, and Dr. Janfred Parpala, lower right, were stationed at Fort Stevens. Following the war, they remained in Astoria and established a practice.

The hospital was built about 1910 in an area known as Hospital Hill, also called "Gobbler's Knob" during the earlier years. Capt. Frederick S. Macy was the post surgeon in 1912. After World War I, contract surgeons were employed for the reduced garrison.

The chapel served all of the residents of the fort and was often the scene of weddings. One resident spoke of seeing a newlywed couple leaving the church atop a caisson. There were also Methodist and Roman Catholic churches in the town of Hammond, just outside the fort's gate.

Fire was always a constant threat. The fire engine was on-call for all emergencies. Shelling practice might set fire to the grass on the dunes, and sparks were a threat to the wooden structures. This USA Hollabird pumper was at Fort Stevens. The trucks were built from the mid- to late 1930s through World War II and were used to protect army bases.

The pumper truck could pump water from the river when necessary for putting out fires. One pumper truck from the fort was given to the town of Hammond when the fort was inactivated.

Daily drills were a part of life on the fort. Repetition improved the soldier's performance and made them ready to be transferred to battles overseas.

War games involved many different practiced events that might be encountered in actual battle situations. Hand-to-hand combat as well as tactical maneuvers were practiced.

Climbing the jungle net was part of the obstacle course.

Troops were transported by cargo truck, and on school days, these trucks also carried the children who lived on base to school.

Jeeps also provided necessary transportation. The Willys Jeep was the basic mode of transportation during World War II.

The half-track, as seen in this spring of 1942 photograph, was quite adept at traversing the dunes. A half-track had regular wheels in the front for steering and caterpillar tracks on the back to propel the vehicle and carry most of the load. The vehicle had the cross-country capabilities of a tank and the handling of a wheeled vehicle.

The motor pool kept all the various vehicles at the fort in operational order. Official cars, in addition to the trucks, jeeps, and other vehicles, were in constant need of maintenance. Sergeant Shultz is wearing the helmet, and Sgt. Keith Roberts is on the right. Both were part of Headquarters Battery 249th of the U.S. Coast Artillery Corps.

In January 1942, these men stopped for a minute for a group photograph. From left to right are Pvt. George Wong, Sgt. William A. Bentson, Private Itzkowitz, and Private Noeta.

Paul F. Laughman stands in a crater made by a projectile fired from a Japanese submarine on the night of June 21, 1942. This crater was about 100 yards southwest of big gun No. 12 at Battery Russell. Three or four were fired, the others landing farther south and busting into pieces.

Five large craters were found in the area after the shelling.

This projectile was set up as a monument to the excellent marksmanship with the 10-inch guns at Battery Russell. The names of the members of the battery are written on the projectile.

Sentiment about World War II can be seen expressed on this sign erected by the soldiers in the barbed wire surrounding Battery Russell.

Other signs posted around the base created a bit of levity during the stressful times and also stated ownership of various places. Stumpy's Tavern was next to little eight-man houses behind the level ground of Battery Russell for the crews of the 10-inch guns.

This group of Arkansas National Guard stands in formation at the fort in 1951. Even after deactivation, the fort was often the site of activity by visiting troops.

Almost resembling a ghost town, the barracks stood empty when the soldiers had departed. The alley at the rear of the west barracks stands waiting for a new group of inhabitants.

The baseball fields continued to host games, and there was even a team that wore the Fort Stevens name in 1938.

In an aerial photograph after the snow fell on the administrative area are pictured the officers' and noncommissioned officers' housing surrounding the parade ground.

Six

FORT STEVENS TODAY

This sign outside the museum
in the historic park gives a brief
introduction to the area.

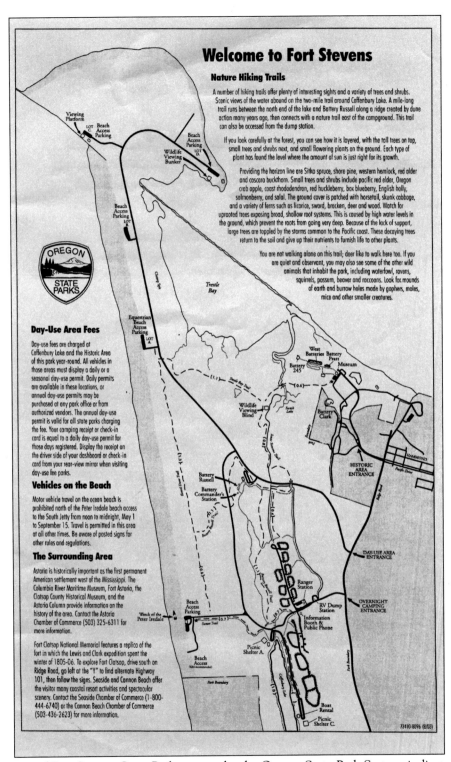

Welcome to Fort Stevens

Nature Hiking Trails

A number of hiking trails offer plenty of interesting sights and a variety of trees and shrubs. Scenic views of the water abound on the two-mile trail around Coffenbury Lake. A mile-long trail runs between the north end of the lake and Battery Russell along a ridge created by dune action many years ago, then connects with a nature trail east of the campground. This trail can also be accessed from the dump station.

If you look carefully at the forest, you can see how it is layered, with the tall trees on top, small trees and shrubs next, and small flowering plants on the ground. Each type of plant has found the level where the amount of sun is just right for its growth.

Providing the horizon line are Sitka spruce, shore pine, western hemlock, red alder and cascara buckthorn. Small trees and shrubs include pacific red elder, Oregon crab apple, coast rhododendron, red huckleberry, box blueberry, English holly, salmonberry, and salal. The ground cover is patched with horsetail, skunk cabbage, and a variety of ferns such as licorice, sword, bracken, deer and wood. Watch for uprooted trees exposing broad, shallow root systems. This is caused by high water levels in the ground, which prevent the roots from going very deep. Because of the lack of support, large trees are toppled by the storms common to the Pacific coast. These decaying trees return to the soil and give up their nutrients to furnish life to other plants.

You are not walking alone on this trail; deer like to walk here too. If you are quiet and observant, you may also see some of the other wild animals that inhabit the park, including waterfowl, ravens, squirrels, possum, beaver and raccoons. Look for mounds of earth and burrow holes made by gophers, moles, mice and other smaller creatures.

Day-Use Area Fees

Day-use fees are charged at Coffenbury Lake and the Historic Area of this park year-round. All vehicles in those areas must display a daily or a seasonal day-use permit. Daily permits are available in these locations, or annual day-use permits may be purchased at any park office or from authorized vendors. The annual day-use permit is valid for all state parks charging the fee. Your camping receipt or check-in card is equal to a daily day-use permit for those days registered. Display the receipt on the driver side of your dashboard or check-in card from your rear-view mirror when visiting day-use fee parks.

Vehicles on the Beach

Motor vehicle travel on the ocean beach is prohibited north of the Peter Iredale beach access to the South Jetty from noon to midnight, May 1 to September 15. Travel is permitted in this area at all other times. Be aware of posted signs for other rules and regulations.

The Surrounding Area

Astoria is historically important as the first permanent American settlement west of the Mississippi. The Columbia River Maritime Museum, Fort Astoria, the Clatsop County Historical Museum, and the Astoria Column provide information on the history of the area. Contact the Astoria Chamber of Commerce (503) 325-6311 for more information.

Fort Clatsop National Memorial features a replica of the fort in which the Lewis and Clark expedition spent the winter of 1805-06. To explore Fort Clatsop, drive south on Ridge Road, go left at the "Y" to find alternate Highway 101, then follow the signs. Seaside and Cannon Beach offer the visitor many coastal resort activities and spectacular scenery. Contact the Seaside Chamber of Commerce (1-800-444-6740) or the Cannon Beach Chamber of Commerce (503-436-2623) for more information.

This map of Fort Stevens State Park, put out by the Oregon State Park System, indicates the hiking trails and historic buildings as they exist today. (Courtesy of Oregon State Parks.)

Duty Through War and Peace
Old Fort Stevens Historic Sit

This sign, near the museum in the historic area, highlights several of the prominent buildings. All of the remaining batteries and buildings also are posted with signs and descriptive information.

Driving through the entrance to Fort Stevens Historical Park, one will pass remnants of the fort. The commissary was built in 1900. All that remains behind the sign and the vast overgrowth is the foundation of the building.

The Test Tanks are next in view on the left. Cables used for the sea mines were tested here before being installed in the river.

The Communications Bunker was a bomb-proof and gas-proof building that served as the center of all communications for the fort. A large switchboard monitored all communications and activities at the fort.

A brick chimney, concrete foundation, and small white sign are all that remain of the many two-story barracks that housed the men stationed here during World War II.

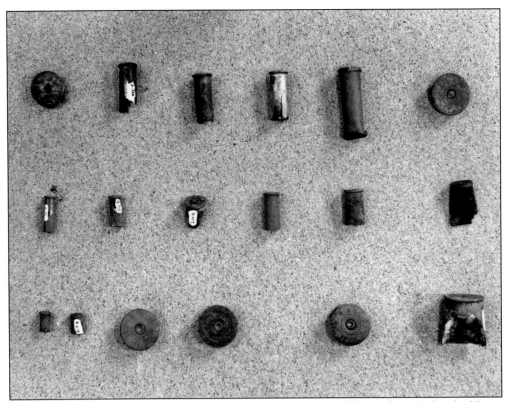

Spent shells from rifles and pistols could be found in the ground long after the fort had been deactivated. Lead balls from black powder rifles and casings from later guns tell of the transition in armament.

The sally port, a reminder of the early years, provides access to the area used for reenactments and living history presentations. Foundations and chimneys are all that remain of the World War II barracks.

Concrete remnants of Battery
Pratt stand quietly waiting for
a tourist's exploration.

No, this is not a smokestack. This
tall tower was the base for the
Battery Pratt command station.
It was filled with cement to give
the platform a stable base.

Visitors can view the original steam plant alongside Batteries West, Walker, and Lewis.

An unarmed submarine mine of the floating type used in the nets on the Columbia River sits ominously along the road.

The submarine mine casement building is only one of the cement structures still standing. Constructed in 1897 and 1898, and inactivated in 1937, it was built to withstand the impact of a 12-inch shell. The original one, of cement covered with sand, was built right next to this remaining building.

Battery Clark remains abandoned except by the birds. In June 1942, Battery Clark was one of two duty batteries the night of the Japanese shelling.

Fiberglass replicas of the 10-inch Rodman cannons stand at the ready. The 10-inch gun fired a 617-pound projectile 16,290 yards with a powder charge of 182 pounds. The Rodman smoothbore cannon Model 1861 U.S. 15-inch columbiad was made of cast iron using the wet chill process. It was named for its inventor, Thomas Jackson Rodman, an 1841 graduate of the West Point Military Academy. The Rodman 15-inch was the largest gun in the U.S. arsenal during the Civil War.

Outside the historic area, the guardhouse stands as a monument to the past. It has been used as a storage facility but is often plagued by flooding.

118

On the outskirts of the historic area near the Columbia River is the torpedo loading area, built around 1900. A metal structure covered the concrete base and tank. Torpedoes were tested in the water tank and then loaded onto railroad cars and taken to the loading dock.

Battery Smur, built in 1902, was named for 3rd Lt. Elias Smur. The battery was armed with two 3-inch rapid-fire guns. Located near the mine casement, it was designed to protect mine operations on the Columbia River. Battery Smur was deactivated in 1920.

Coal once came in by train to be used as fuel for heating the fort buildings. The coal yard also remains long abandoned.

The fort cemetery is still in use and is maintained by the Friends of Old Fort Stevens by contract with the U.S. Department of Defense.

The first burial, held on May 19, 1868, was for Pvt. August Stahlberger of C Company, 2nd Artillery. The first lighthouse keeper at Cape Disappointment, Washington, is also buried here. This is how the cemetery looked in 1978.

Currently, there are approximately 215 graves in the cemetery, and additional burials continue to occur.

This 155-millimeter gun was used in both World War I and World War II. Although on display here, it was never used at Fort Stevens.

Scott Geren, a member of the board of Friends of Old Fort Stevens, built this Jeep from scrap metal for children to climb on and for photographic opportunities. It is parked outside the museum.

In front of the museum is the memorial rose garden. Many families and friends of those who were stationed here have roses planted in their memory. Each plant is identified as to the variety and the person for whom it was planted.

The museum store has books and other memorabilia for sale.

Visitors come to view reenactments of Civil War and World War II battles held in the park during the summer, in addition to visiting the museum. Many visitors also choose to tour the park in a 1950s GMC 2.5-ton cargo truck.

Encampments of soldiers from the Civil War are erected on the field near the museum, bringing the fort to life. Tents, uniforms, and guns of the era complete the scene.

Down another road to the south of the historic area is Battery Russell. This battery is the site of the annual exhibit commemorating the shelling of Fort Stevens on June 21, 1942. In the 1930s, Japanese merchantmen off scrap ships visited the fort and took pictures. Perhaps these pictures later assisted the Japanese with the fort's location for the shelling.

Although the guns have been removed, the pits where they were located remain. Planners thought it would have been wiser to place 12-inch guns here because the guns on ships had greater range, but the battery was already under construction, and it was too late to make the change.

Battery Russell is the site of the Pacific Rim Peace Memorial. On it is written: "Pacific Rim Peace Memorial dedicated to members of the 249th Coast Artillery, Oregon National Guard; the 18th Coast Artillery Corps Regiment; Headquarters Harbor Defenses of the Columbia River and all other United States personnel stationed at Fort Stevens, Fort Canby, Fort Columbia, C.A.S.C.U. No.1924 and the crew of the Japanese Submarine I-25. / Near this place on the night of June 21, 1942, they faced each other when the Japanese submarine shelled Fort Stevens, making it the first foreign attack on a continental military installation since the War of 1812. / May peace between our nations be everlasting [also written in Japanese]. / Dedicated June 21, 1992."

Each September there is a reunion of soldiers who served at the fort. Pictured from left to right are (first row) Charles Talley, Donald Moy, Maynard Miller, Bob Swaggert, Clarence Thayer, and Pat Jordan; (second row) Hubert Adkins, Bob Goodman, Warren Poling, Eric Fitzsimmons, Bill Gilley and two unidentified; (third row) Chad Parsons, Jeff White, Larry Martin, and unidentified.

DISCOVER THOUSANDS OF LOCAL HISTORY BOOKS FEATURING MILLIONS OF VINTAGE IMAGES

Arcadia Publishing, the leading local history publisher in the United States, is committed to making history accessible and meaningful through publishing books that celebrate and preserve the heritage of America's people and places.

Find more books like this at
www.arcadiapublishing.com

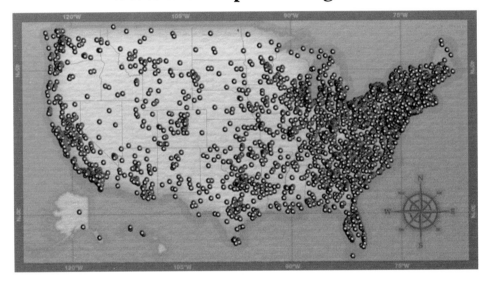

Search for your hometown history, your old stomping grounds, and even your favorite sports team.